Marine Nina Denis & Flora Denis

DIY for Witches

Make 22 Objects for Daily Magical Practice

Photography by Benoit Beghyn

stashBOOKS®

an imprint of C&T Publishing

Contents

Part 3 ◊ MAGIC RESOURCES

Introduction

Surrounding yourself with the right tools is essential when practicing magic. In this book, you will find DIY magical objects that will accompany you in your daily life, in your practice, and during your rituals.

Our magical and ritual objects are personal tools. Each of them must be welcomed with mindfulness. A real connection must be created so that they become an extension of ourselves.

An encounter, even love at first sight, must occur between you and the object. This can happen when browsing in a store, but also at a flea market or a garage sale. Or it can happen with an object received as a gift from a loved one.

But in our opinion, the most effective tool will be one that you have taken the time to lovingly craft and with which you have established a genuine connection, from the moment of its conception.

In this book, you will discover easy-to-make tools that will be useful in your everyday magical work and your rituals.

These DIY projects are the product of our own experience. Feel free to adapt them as you see fit, though be careful, especially regarding the use of plants and essential oils. We encourage you to learn more about their contraindications before use.

Test, invent, experiment, and trust your own magic.

Flora and Marine

Part 1

·⟡·

YOUR MAGICAL OBJECTS

Your Everyday Magical Objects

When you practice magic, you must surround
yourself with certain essential objects that will
accompany you both in everyday life as well as
in your works and rituals.

These items must be carefully selected, as they will become extensions of
yourself. They are strictly personal and must be pampered and regularly
maintained in order for their effectiveness to remain intact.

Rest assured: If you are just starting out, you don't need to acquire
everything immediately. Give yourself time to get to know your tools.
The process can take several months or even several years.

You can craft most of them yourself. This will increase their power and
strengthen the connection between you.

The Witch's Essential Tools

In the second part of this book, you will find step-by-step DIY projects for creating tools that will serve you daily in your magical work. We've selected in advance the essential tools you will need in order to effectively practice, and you can make almost all of them yourself.

THE WAND

The wand is used to channel energy during a ritual. It must be made by the witch or warlock who possesses it (see Magic Wand, page 80).

THE BOOK OF SHADOWS / GRIMOIRE

The Book of Shadows is a notebook for recording the recipes and results of all your personal practices. It represents your memory as a witch or warlock. Traditionally, upon the death of its owner, it is passed on to his or her descendants or burned if there are no heirs. You can use any notebook as a Book of Shadows, but it will be much more personal and powerful if you craft it yourself (see Book of Shadows, page 108).

THE CAULDRON

The well-known magic cauldron is used to burn incense or plants. It can also be used as a divination tool when filled with water. Today you can find small cast-iron cauldrons in esoteric shops, but you can also substitute a bowl or a saucepan.

THE PENTACLE

A pentacle is a disc representing a star and used during consecration rituals. It is also an essential element of the altar. You can find them in esoteric shops, but it is a very simple tool to make yourself (see Pentacle, page 76).

THE CANDLE

Candles are as helpful in your daily life as they are in your rituals. Colored candles allow you to establish a particular intention (see The Meaning of Colors, page 142). You can also use white candles enhanced with essential oils or plants to diffuse their properties (see Magic Candles, page 32). We recommend that you always check candles' ingredients before using them. Commercially available candles, especially inexpensive ones like tea lights, can be harmful. Opt instead for natural materials, such as soy wax (which has a delicious natural scent of vanilla) or beeswax.

THE SMOKE CLEANSING STICK

This is a bundle of dried plants that has always been used to purify places, whether in the traditions of indigenous peoples or in Western medicine. It is now a staple in modern magic (see Smoke Cleansing Stick, page 84).

THE CHALICE

This stemmed cup will be used to drink water, wine, or cider during rituals. Traditionally, this is a silver goblet decorated with magical symbols, but you can just as easily use a simple stemmed glass, which will become your chalice.

THE ALTAR

The altar is the sacred space on which to place ritual objects, elements found in nature, candles, or whatever you wish to put there to symbolize your practice. It will be used to set the intentions of the moment and will change according to your mood, the seasons, and the festivals (see Pagan Festivals for Rituals, page 134). It can be big or small, for all to see or tucked away in a small corner, depending on your needs and desires.

THE ATHAME

The athame is a dagger used to draw magic circles during rituals. It is also used when gathering, to cut the plants which will serve you in your magical work.

Purifying and Charging
Your Magical Objects

Whether you use your magical items everyday or only for rituals, you must regularly cleanse and charge them to maintain their full effectiveness.

PURIFYING

One of the simplest techniques for purifying an object is the technique of smoke cleansing, using bundles of dried plants (see Smoke Cleansing Stick, page 84) or incense.

Light your stick and diffuse its smoke by circling counterclockwise around the object at least three times. Visualize the object free of all the energies that are not useful to it. Trust your feelings as to when to stop the smoke cleansing.

When should you purify your objects?
✧ Before and after a magical ritual or work.
✧ When you acquire a new item.
✧ If the object has been touched or used by someone other than yourself.
✧ For regular maintenance: about once a month or whenever you feel the need.

Caution: Using a smoke cleansing stick is not recommended in the presence of children, pregnant women, or people with respiratory problems.

What objects can be purified?
Almost any item can be purified. There are no contraindications. You can also purify places or people using the same technique.

CHARGING

After being purified, some items need to be charged to increase their effectiveness. One of the simplest techniques is to charge them in the light of the full moon.

During a full moon, place your objects outside for a few hours or place them by a window so that the moonlight can reach them.

If the object is small, you can also place it in the center of a scallop shell. This will charge it naturally.

When should you charge your items?
✧ Before a magical ritual or work.
✧ When you acquire a new item.
✧ If the object has been touched or used by someone other than yourself.
✧ For regular maintenance: about once a month or whenever you feel the need.

Remember: Don't forget to purify your items before charging them.

What objects can be charged?
✧ Stones and crystals
✧ Amulets and talismans
✧ Pentacles
✧ Wish boxes
✧ Magic wands
✧ Magic brooms
✧ Pendulums
✧ Runes
✧ Oracles
✧ Cauldrons
✧ Athames
✧ Chalices
✧ And many others...

Crafting

Our magical objects are extensions of ourselves. Crafting them is an essential step in creating a strong bond with them. You must therefore prepare for crafting meticulously and then work with as much intention as you would in a ritual.

For the DIY projects presented in this book, we have chosen natural elements that you will be able to find in nature and materials readily available in stores. They should be selected with care, as they are the raw materials for your magical items.

Once your creations have been made, to complete the process and to increase their effectiveness, we recommend that you consecrate them before their first use.

Choosing the Right Materials

Crafting your items is an essential step in your magical process. For greater effectiveness, each constituent element must be selected with care and respect for nature.

NATURE

Nature is the first place to go when looking for the raw materials to use when crafting your magical objects. In this book, many projects contain elements that you can find in the woods or on the beach.

When you need to cut plants (for example, for an herbarium, smoke cleansing stick, botanical pillow, plant hanging, or magic vial), only pick those that you can identify with certainty. There are many similarities between those that are edible and those that are poisonous. Make sure you never pick any protected species. Also, only gather what you need and only remove the roots if necessary. You can harvest your plants by using your athame, a knife, scissors, or a brush hook, preferably with a wooden handle. To avoid damaging the harvested plants, transport them in a dedicated cotton bag or a box. Avoid crushing or smothering your plants before drying.

If you need to collect branches (for a magic wand, pentacle, moon mobile, or magic broom), choose those that have fallen to the ground. If at all possible, avoid directly cutting a tree.

For all elements collected in nature, be careful not to gather them in sensitive and protected natural areas.

ORGANIC SHOPS

To obtain plants that you have not found in nature, if possible, get them directly from a producer of aromatic and medicinal plants. You can also buy your dried plants from organic stores or herbalists. Avoid plants that have been stored with exposure to light (in transparent packaging). For fresh plants, go to organic stores (or produce markets). There you will also find essential oils for making candles and salts.

FLORISTS

Some projects require a large number of flowers (especially the Flower Crown), and if you can't find them in the wild, check with your florist. If possible, choose a fair-trade florist who sells locally grown flowers and respects seasonality. The flowers will travel less and contain fewer chemicals, making them more effective.

HOBBY AND CRAFT STORES

Most of the remaining items can be found in craft stores. Here too, we encourage you to check the origin of your raw materials. The less distance they have traveled, the more effective they will be. For wool, opt for organic wool. For wax, choose domestic soy wax.

COSMETICS STORES

For making magic salts, we recommend you use oxide, available in specialty stores selling materials for homemade cosmetics, where you can also obtain essential oils for candles. Choose organic essential oils or those with environmental certification.

Crafting Ritual

For optimal power, the crafting of each magical object should be prepared as a ritual. This preparation is an important step for the future effectiveness of the object.

1. Clean the space
Clean the crafting space. Make sure that the room in which you will be working is clean and airy. You can also cleanse its energy by burning a smoke cleansing stick around your crafting space.

2. Clean your tools
Purify each tool that will be used in the crafting of your magical object, using a smoke cleansing stick.

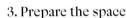

3. Prepare the space
Place in front of you all the tools that will be used in crafting your magical object, and thank them before starting your work. As with a classic ritual, you can arrange candles around your workspace to reinforce and channel the action.

4. Set your intention
Before embarking on the crafting of your object, establish an intention for its use. Visualize the finished product and imagine the different ways it will serve you.

5. Craft in mindfulness
You can now get started. Throughout the crafting of your object, keep its future benefits in mind. Be fully present in every step of the crafting process. Feel the bond that is created with the object. If your mind wanders, bring it back to what you are doing.

6. Welcome your object
Once your crafting is complete, thank all your tools and greet the new object by welcoming it.

Consecrating Your Magical Objects

Every object used in magical work or rituals must be consecrated when it comes into our possession and before it is used for the first time. We provide instructions here for consecrating objects according to the four elements.

WHAT YOU WILL NEED

◊ 1 smoke-cleansing stick or incense
   (for the air element)
◊ 1 white candle
   (for the fire element)
◊ 1 bowl of water
   (for the water element)
◊ Salt on a plate
   (for the earth element)

1. Place yourself within a magic circle that you have drawn on the ground.

2. Pass the object 3 times through the smoke of the smoke cleansing stick.

3. Pass the object 3 times through the flame of the candle (or above the flame if the object is flammable).

4. Pour 3 drops of water onto the object.

5. Place the object on the salt.

6. Take the object in your hands and visualize its magical function.

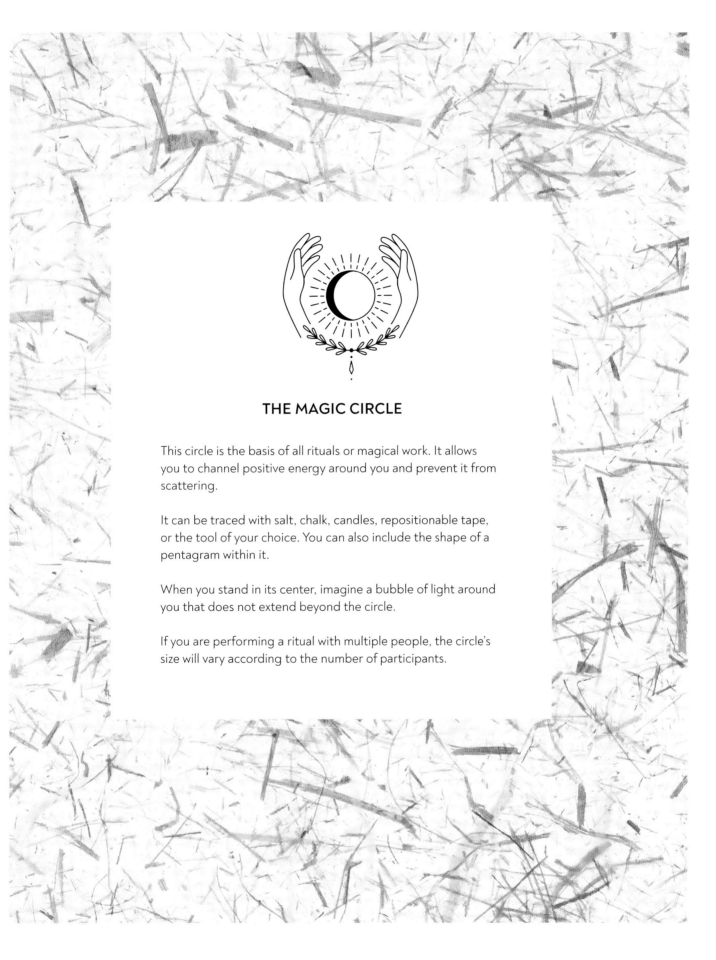

THE MAGIC CIRCLE

This circle is the basis of all rituals or magical work. It allows you to channel positive energy around you and prevent it from scattering.

It can be traced with salt, chalk, candles, repositionable tape, or the tool of your choice. You can also include the shape of a pentagram within it.

When you stand in its center, imagine a bubble of light around you that does not extend beyond the circle.

If you are performing a ritual with multiple people, the circle's size will vary according to the number of participants.

Part 2

·✦·

DIY

Magical Home

In this chapter, we present DIY instructions for turning your home into a magical cocoon.

Wherever we live is our witch or warlock cocoon. We must feel connected and in harmony with it. It is the place where we rest, recharge, and protect ourselves from the outside world, but also, very often, where we practice our magical work. We have to make sure we pamper it and maintain its balance.

When you have the option, be sure to choose your living space mindfully. Trust your intuition when visiting an apartment or a house. Do you feel welcome and comfortable? Learn about its previous occupants and its history.

Before settling there, consider cleaning it from top to bottom and purifying its energy. Introduce yourself to your new living space and welcome it with kindness.

If you'd like to practice your magic within your home, it is best to consecrate a room to it. We realize, however, that this is often difficult. In this case, select a small corner to establish your altar, on which you can place your magical objects.

Magic Candles

Arranged in a circle, candles allow energy to be channeled during a ritual. Used alone, they help us to set an intention.

Candles symbolize the four complementary energies: air, with the oxygen that feeds the candle's flame; earth, represented by the candle in its solid state; water, when the wax becomes liquid; and fire, when the wick is lit. Indispensable companions of all magical work, they are placed in a circle during rituals to channel energy into the center. They are also of great help during meditation and visualization exercises or in setting an intention. Lastly, in everyday life, they can make your evenings cozier while providing you with their benefits.

Magical Advice

To extinguish a candle after magical work, do not blow directly on it. This cuts off the energy released during your practice. You can use a snuffer or a little water.

WHAT YOU WILL NEED

◊ 250g (8.8oz) of soy wax
◊ 20 drops of essential oils
◊ 1 wax-coated candle wick

◊ A 20cl (6.8oz) glass jar
◊ A few pinches of dried plants

CAUTION

When the candle is completely consumed, the dried plants may continue to burn. Do not let the candle burn all the way down. Extinguish it when a few millimeters (about ¼in) of wax remain. In any situation, never leave a candle burning unattended.

1. Heat your soy wax in a double boiler until it reaches 70°C (158°F). Then pour the essential oils and wax into a container and mix.

2. Place the wick at the bottom of the glass jar, using a little hot wax to fix it in place. Then pour the wax and essential oil mixture into the glass jar.

3. Wait for the candle to set slightly, then sprinkle it with dried plants.

You can use chopsticks or a clothespin to hold the wick in the center of your candle.

RECIPES

Concentration and Energy
10 drops of peppermint essential oil · 10 drops of rosemary essential oil · 1 pinch of dried mint · 1 pinch of dried rosemary

Protection and Purification
10 drops of myrrh essential oil · 10 drops of true or spike lavender essential oil · 1 pinch of dried sage · 1 pinch of dried lavender flowers

Divination and Clairvoyance
10 drops of orange essential oil · 10 drops of tarragon essential oil · A few grams (about 0.14oz) of dried orange peel · 1 pinch of dried rosemary

Love and Self-Confidence
15 drops of ylang ylang essential oil · 5 drops of clove essential oil · 1 dried and crumbled rose petal · 1 pinch of dried mint

Relaxation and Meditation
10 drops of frankincense essential oil · 10 drops of marjoram essential oil · A few dried chamomile flowers · A few dried and crumbled verbena leaves

Note: The use of these essential oil candles is not recommended in the presence of pregnant women or young children.

TO GO FURTHER

You can also add color to your candles with natural pigments, depending on the magical work you need to perform. Each color has its specific power, which will complete the intention you set with the candle and its ingredients (see The Meaning of Colors, page 142).

Magic Wallhanging

Crafted with mindfulness, your magic wallhanging forms a visual representation of a request or intention that you want to keep close to you.

The knot symbolizes union and liberation. In many traditions, it represents both a connection between the human and the divine and one between the human and the elements. Throughout the knot-designing process for your wallhanging, develop a specific intention or request that you wish to see manifested. Thus charged with your energy, your creation becomes an intimate work that will find its place above your altar or any room of your home. You can also offer a wallhanging to the person of your choice, with a benevolent intention set for them.

TIP

You can choose to use a cord with a different diameter or make a wallhanging with several different cords. If doing this, consider adapting the size of your stick and of the cord pieces. The thicker the cord and/or the more knots you have, the longer the cords and the larger the stick needed.

Magical Advice

If this is your first wallhanging, take the time to practice tying knots so that the movement becomes almost automatic. The more accustomed to the movement you become, the better you can concentrate on the intentions to be set in the work.

WHAT YOU WILL NEED

◊ 1 stick about 35cm (13¾in) long
◊ 1 pair of scissors
◊ 1 spool of combed or twisted cotton macrame cord

Feel free to consult the table in The Meaning of Colors (page 142) when choosing your cord.

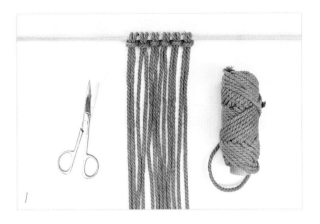

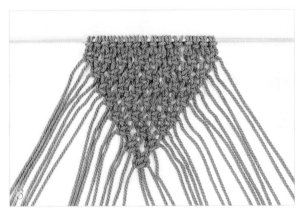

1. Cut 16 lengths of cord 2m (2⅛yds) long. Tie them next to each other following diagram A (page 39).

2. Along the entire length, make a series of knots following diagram B. Then make a series of knots below them following diagram C.

3. Repeat Step 2 for each row. To give your wallhanging the shape of a triangle: Keep 2 unknotted cords at the beginning of the row and 2 more at the end of the row. Then keep 4 on each end of the next row, then 6 (and so on).

4. Once the rows are complete, tie the cords at the ends of the rows to the cords from the row below. In the last row, tie the cords behind the knot following diagrams B and C.

HOW TO TIE THE KNOTS

Diagram A

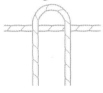   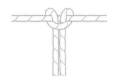

Place the folded cord over the stick.
Pull the loop behind the stick.
Insert both ends into the loop.
Pull the ends to tighten the knot.

Diagram B

 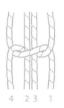

Place cord 1 over cords 2 and 3, then under cord 4.
Place cord 4 under cords 3 and 2, then over cord 1.
Pull the ends to position the knot.

Diagram C

Again, place cord 1 over cords 3 and 2, and under cord 4.
Then place cord 4 under 2 and 3 and come out through the loop.
Pull cords 1 and 4 to tighten them.

TO GO FURTHER

Depending on your inspiration, feel free to use several colors to craft your wallhanging. You can also decorate it with wooden beads or hang feathers from the end of the cords. Let your creativity lead the way.

Botanical Pillow

The plant cushion is a pillow made of dried plants, crafted to use during sleep or during your meditation and yoga practices.

The botanical pillow will be by your side at night to soothe your sleep or to promote the frequency and recollection of your dreams. It can also be made for your meditation or active practices. In each of these situations, the choice of plants is fundamental. Below, we provide mixtures based on the properties of plants. However, don't be afraid to formulate your own recipes by referring to List of the Magical Powers of Plants (page 138).

RECIPES

✧ *Deep Sleep*
Poppy · Lavender · Rose · Verbena · Salt

✧ *Vivid Dreams*
Mugwort · Poppy · Bird's-foot trefoil · Peony · Salt

✧ *Deep Meditation*
Basil · Sage · Mint · Laurel (bay leaf) · Salt

✧ *Yoga*
Eucalyptus · Sage · Rosemary · Mint · Salt

Magical Advice

The magical effect of the botancial cushion remains as long as the plants are fragrant. When there is no longer any fragrance present, empty the pillow and prepare a new mixture.

WHAT YOU WILL NEED

◊ Dried plants, representing 50% of the total stuffing
◊ Grain husks (millet, spelt, or buckwheat), representing 50% of the total stuffing
◊ 1 cotton pillowcase, preferably with a zip closure
(recommended size: 30 × 50cm [11¾in × 19⅝in] or 40 × 40cm [15¾in × 15¾in])
◊ 1 pinch of salt

We have not specified a quantity for dried plants and grain stuffing, as it depends on the density of the plants selected and whether you prefer a softer or firmer pillow.

1. In a large bowl, combine the dried plants and grain husks.

2. Insert everything into the pillowcase. Adjust the amount if necessary. Add a pinch of salt for its protective power.

3. Verbalize your intention depending on how you will use your botanical pillow. Then close the pillowcase.

TO GO FURTHER

To give your botanical pillow extra power, embroider it with a magical sign or symbol (see Magical Signs and Symbols, page 144).

Herbarium

The herbarium is a crucial study tool; it forms the most significant part of the plant memory of different peoples.

As you continue to practice magic, you will probably come to gather your plants yourself. At that time, creating an herbarium will allow you to keep a lasting record of your harvests by noting in this tool which species you have discovered, as well as where and when you collected them. You will then be able to schedule and optimize your future harvests while keeping the magical influence of your plants close at hand. Your herbarium should be stored away from light and humidity.

Magical Advice

GATHERING PLANTS

It is preferable to harvest plants in dry weather; plants should not be wet when you place them to dry. While gathering, make sure never to collect protected species or to harvest them in sensitive or protected natural areas. Furthermore, be sure to gather only what you need and only remove the roots if necessary. To avoid damaging the harvested plants, transport them in a dedicated cotton bag or box, and avoiding crushing or smothering them before drying. Along the way, give nature a boost by scattering a few seeds from your harvest. Remember to thank the gathered plants and the earth for its gifts.

WHAT YOU WILL NEED

◊ Some freshly gathered plants
◊ Newspaper or sheets of blotting paper
◊ 1 thick book
◊ 1 pair of scissors
◊ 1 journal or notebook (preferably closed with an elastic band)
◊ Glue or self-adhesive paper

1. Arrange the plants one by one to dry between 2 sheets of newspaper or blotting paper. Place them between 2 pages of a thick book for 2 to 3 weeks.

2. After they have dried, glue the plants in your notebook using a small dot of glue or small strips of adhesive paper. Avoid tape, as its adhesive is too strong.

3. For each plant inserted, note the name of the species, location, and date of harvest. You can also personalize your herbarium with sketches.

DID YOU KNOW?

Many plant species recorded in nineteenth- and twentieth-century herbariums have now disappeared or have been replaced by others. Therefore, if you pass it on, your herbarium can be a very interesting tool for generations to come.

Plant Hangings

Very popular in green magic, hanging is a particularly effective technique for optimizing the drying of your plants.

After a wild harvest or the acquisition of fresh plants (intended, for example, for crafting your perpetual Flower Crown, page 96), the plants must be completely dried to preserve them without affecting their powers. There are several techniques for doing this, such as drying on racks or using a dehydrator. However, hanging remains the most efficient and practical tool for drying small quantities of plants.

WHAT YOU WILL NEED

◊ Bunches of freshly cut plants
◊ Cotton or hemp string
◊ 1 branch or 1 wooden stick about 80cm (31½in) long

1. Prepare loose bunches so that the drying is optimal. Tie them together with cotton or hemp string. Leave about 50cm (19⅝in) of string.

2. Cut a 1m (1yd) length of string. Tie the ends 5cm (2in) from each end of the wooden stick. Hang the stick from the string.

3. On the hanging stick, attach the bunches of plants upside down, spaced 10cm (3⅞in) apart. You can optimize the space by varying the lengths of string in order to hang your plants in a staggered fashion.

PRECAUTIONS

✧ If the plants are to be eaten, clean them thoroughly before drying.

✧ Avoid direct light exposure so that plants do not lose their properties and colors.

✧ Once dry, your plants can be stored, for culinary preparations or herbal teas, for several months in an airtight jar away from humidity and light.

Magical Advice

What uses are there for my dried plants?

Herbal Teas
Let the plants steep for 5 to 15 minutes in simmering water, depending on the quantity and your taste. Strain and enjoy.

Magical Cooking (or Kitchen Witchery)
Concoct botanical dishes or drinks so that you may benefit from their magical properties through ingestion.

Smoke Cleansing
You can burn plants without necessarily creating a smoke cleansing stick. To do this, in a suitable container, place dried leaves or flowers on glowing charcoal.

Magical Objects
You can use your plants to make magical tools (an amulet, botanical pillow, and the like) or simply to make bouquets.

Moon Mobile

A decorative object for a magical interior, the moon mobile reminds us daily of our connection with this heavenly body.

The moon is an essential partner in the daily life of any witch or warlock. Its cyclical character influences nature but also us. Have you ever noticed that you sleep particularly poorly on full moon nights? Or that your menstrual period has the same number of days as the moon's cycle? The moon's different phases are essential landmarks during magical rituals and practices.

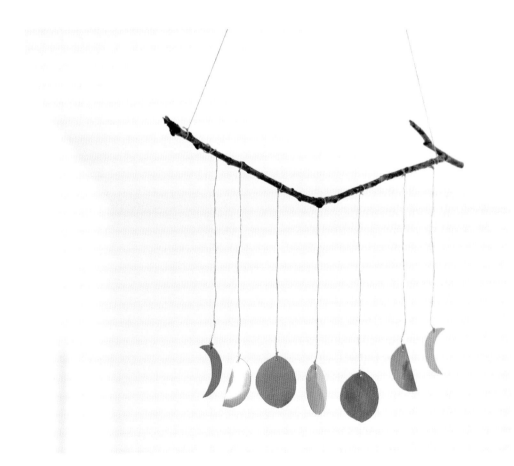

Magical Advice

Write down your intentions for the coming lunar cycle on the shape of a full moon. At each new moon, cut out a new full moon and repeat this action.

WHAT YOU WILL NEED

◊ 1 ball of string
◊ 1 wooden stick about 80cm (31½in) long
◊ Tracing paper
◊ 1 pair of scissors

◊ Thick paper of at least 150 g/m² (102 lb), in the color of your choice
◊ 1 craft knife
◊ 1 hole punch

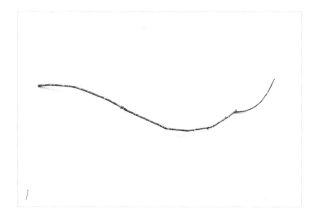

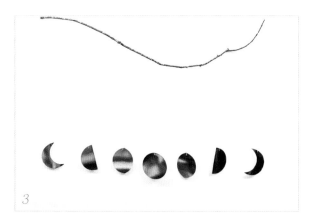

1. Cut a 100cm (39⅜in) length of string and tie the ends 5cm (2in) from each end of the wooden stick. Hang the stick from the string. Then cut 7 pieces of string 30cm (11¾in) long. Tie them to the stick at intervals of 12cm (4¾in).

2. Reproduce the lunar phases shown in Lunar Phases (page 146) on tracing paper. Cut out the shapes of the moons and trace them on the thick paper (1 full moon, 2 crescents, 2 quarters, and 2 gibbous).

3. Cut the moon shapes out of the thick paper. Punch holes in the upper parts. Tie each phase to a string. The full moon will be in the middle, and both sides will follow this order: a gibbous moon, a quarter moon, and last, a crescent moon.

THE LUNAR CYCLE

The lunar phases and associated magical work
or actions:

● *New moon*
Purify yourself, set your intentions.

◑ *Waxing crescent*
Take care of yourself, create.

◗ *First quarter*
Organize, act.

◐ *Waxing gibbous*
Open yourself up to your environment, thank it.

○ *Full moon*
Take action, accomplish your intentions.

◖ *Waning gibbous*
Thank yourself.

◑ *Third quarter*
Close your intentions, complete your actions.

◐ *Waning crescent*
Sort, clean your environment.

Magic on the Go

In this chapter, we present DIY projects to
take your magic with you everywhere.

A stressful day at the office, too much time on public transportation, or
a visit to a place steeped in history are moments when you need a little
magical support.

And since the practice of magic is not constrained within the walls of our
homes, in this chapter we provide DIY objects to accompany you and
protect you wherever you go.

Botanical Amulet

A small pouch filled with dried plants, the botanical amulet is an object that allows you to take the powerful magic of plants everywhere.

Ever present throughout time and in all civilizations, the amulet is a powerful tool to protect the one who wears it or the space where it is placed. The protective amulet takes different forms (statuettes, jewelry, or pieces of paper or fabric), but it can also be intangible and embodied by a sign or a word. The botanical amulet presented here is made up of plants chosen according to their powers. Because of its great purifying power, a pinch of salt is always added to it. The effectiveness of this amulet derives from the quality of the plants used and the power of the intention that you put in it.

Magical Advice

You can choose your plants using a pendulum (page 116) or by drawing cards. Follow your intuition—it's your greatest ally!

WHAT YOU WILL NEED

◊ Some dried plants
◊ 1 small linen or cotton bag, ideally 5 × 5cm (2in × 2in)
◊ Salt
Optional: A small object (stone, jewel, or lock of hair) or a small note of intention to slip into the amulet

---

TO GO FURTHER

A bag made of natural material, such as linen or cotton, allows plants to spread their properties gently and over a long period of time. Feel free to sew the amulet pouch yourself, as this will make it even more effective.

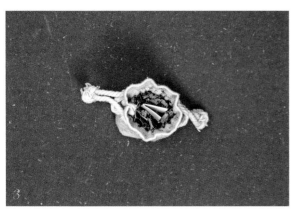

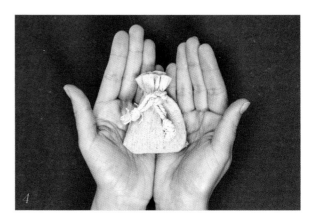

1. Choose your magical plants by referring to Recipes for Botanical Amulets (next page) or List of the Magical Powers of Plants (page 138).

2. In a bowl, make your mixture of plants using 1 to 3 pinches of each ingredient (depending on the size of your bag). Add 1 pinch of salt.

3. Fill the bag with the mixture of plants and salt. If desired, add the small object or folded note.

4. Close the bag with a few stitches or a knot. Verbalize your intention by pronouncing a clear sentence, thus expressing the protective function of the amulet.

DIRECTIONS FOR USE

The amulet's plants will be active as long as they maintain their scent. Rub the sachet between your hands to reactivate the plants when the fragrance fades.

If your amulet gets wet, immediately put it on a heat source.

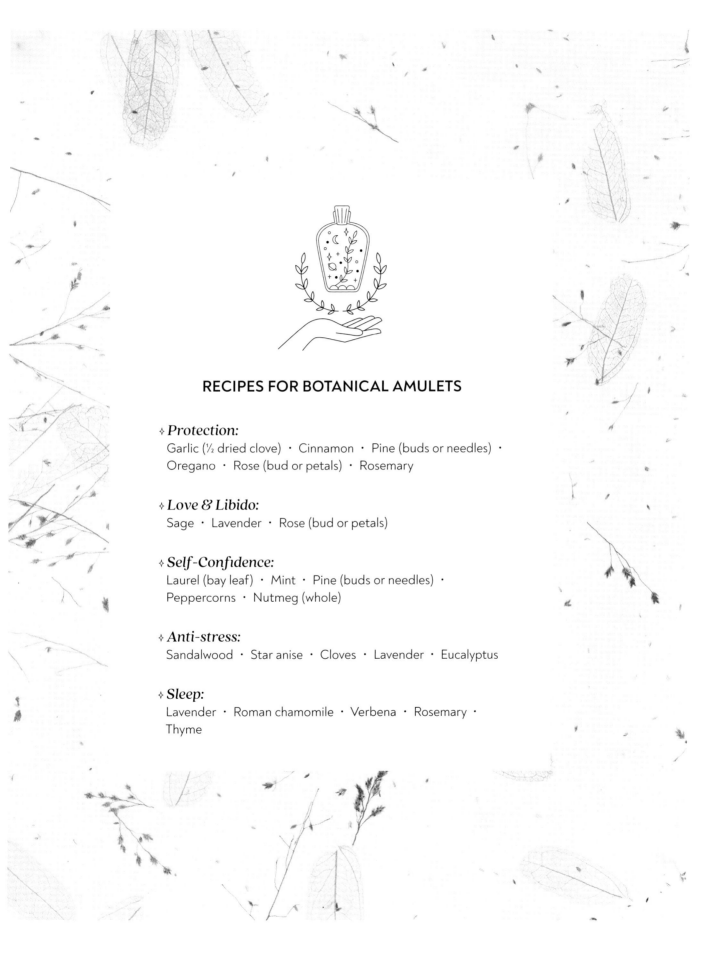

RECIPES FOR BOTANICAL AMULETS

✦ *Protection:*
Garlic (½ dried clove) · Cinnamon · Pine (buds or needles) ·
Oregano · Rose (bud or petals) · Rosemary

✦ *Love & Libido:*
Sage · Lavender · Rose (bud or petals)

✦ *Self-Confidence:*
Laurel (bay leaf) · Mint · Pine (buds or needles) ·
Peppercorns · Nutmeg (whole)

✦ *Anti-stress:*
Sandalwood · Star anise · Cloves · Lavender · Eucalyptus

✦ *Sleep:*
Lavender · Roman chamomile · Verbena · Rosemary ·
Thyme

Magic Vial

Beautiful and poetic, the magic vial contains an eternal plant that will decorate your home's interior or that you can wear around your neck.

Have you fallen in love with the beauty and benefits of a small flower? This project allows you to capture it in a small vial and keep it that way forever. This small, minimalist, and delicate object can be mounted as a pendant, used to decorate your home, or placed on your desk so that you always have a little of the magic of plants with you.

WHAT YOU WILL NEED

◊ 1 small glass vial 1–1.5cm (⅜in–⅝in) wide and
    2–7cm (¾in–2¾in) high, with 1 cork stopper
◊ 1 sprig of a fresh or dried plant
◊ 1 pair of gloves
◊ 1 uncolored epoxy resin kit for crafting, composed
    of 2 bottles (Phases A and B)

◊ 1 syringe
◊ 70% rubbing alcohol
◊ Strong glue
◊ 1 screw eye with a 4mm (⅛in) diameter ring (if you
    wish to wear it as a pendant)

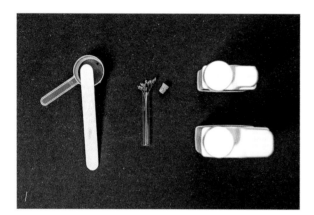

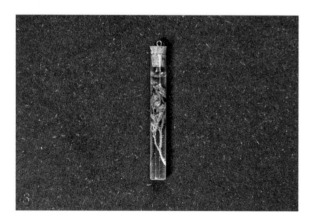

TIP

If you're using a fresh plant, we recommend
that you clean and dry it thoroughly before its
inclusion in the resin.

1. Place your plant in the clean, dry vial. Put on the gloves. In a small container, mix exactly 1 part of the epoxy
   resin of phase B with 2 parts of phase A.

2. Using the syringe, inject the resulting mixture into the vial. Place the vial to dry for 24 hours, left open and
   protected from dust. Thoroughly clean all your tools with the alcohol.

3. After 24 hours have passed, you can close the vial with the cork stopper, adding a dab of strong glue so that
   the two do not separate. Screw the screw eye into the cork stopper.

TO GO FURTHER

You can do the same project in a small silicone mold. Let dry 24 hours before removing from the mold. This will produce a small decorative plant object.

Wish Box

The wish box will be used to set
intentions that you want to see come true.

All magical acts are meant to manifest an intention. Whether it is through crafting an object or practicing ritual or magical work, the goal is to shape and influence energies, in collaboration with the spiritual world, to direct them toward a particular intention. The wish box makes it possible to set an intention for something that we would like to see come true and to project it so that it can be manifested.

WHAT YOU WILL NEED

◊ 1 small box made of wood or matchsticks
◊ Acrylic paint
◊ 1 paintbrush
◊ 1 small sheet of paper or parchment (page 92)
◊ 1 pen
◊ Some small objects of your choice (see To Go Further, page 69)

1. Paint the box with one or more colors that are meaningful to you (see The Meaning of Colors, page 142). You can also include magical designs (see Magical Signs and Symbols, page 144).

2. Write the wish of your choice or an intention on the paper or parchment. Place it in the box, perhaps accompanied by small objects. Close the box and place it in a dark place until the wish is fulfilled.

Magical Advice

Wish Box Consecration Ritual

Once painted, place your open wish box in front of you. Arrange around it a smoke cleansing or incense stick, a cup of water, a bowl of salt, and a white candle. Cleanse your box using the smoke from the stick, put a few drops of water and a few grains of salt on the bottom of the box, and light the candle. Once consecrated, your box is energized for three months or for the fulfillment of three wishes. Repeat the ritual after this period to continue using the box.

TO GO FURTHER

You can slip small objects into the box to reinforce your intention:

For any wish
A strand of your own hair or the hair of the person you're wishing for.

Love
A few rose petals.

Luck
A dried clove of garlic.

Healing
A sprig of thyme or rosemary.

Money
A coin or a bill.

Protection
A pinch of salt.

Friendship
A piece of dried apple.

Reconciliation
A white ribbon.

Progress, leaving the past behind
A small amount of earth.

Talisman

The talisman is a companion to slip in your pocket and take everywhere with you for reassurance, protection, and to help you overcome the little tribulations of everyday life.

The talisman is a sacred object that can take different forms (a stone, ring, jewel, or paper). It is used for protection, security, happiness, wish fulfillment, or to accompany us in our accomplishments (such as love, luck, or self-confidence). It can be found in many belief systems. It is also a precious ally in all forms of magic. The power of a talisman is inextricably linked with the person it belongs to and, like all magical items, its power is increased tenfold when it is made by the wearer. With this project, we present a talisman made from a stone found in nature, and through this talisman you can form an intention or a wish according to your needs.

WHAT YOU WILL NEED

◊ 1 small stone found in nature
◊ Acrylic paint and 1 paintbrush, or 1 paint pen

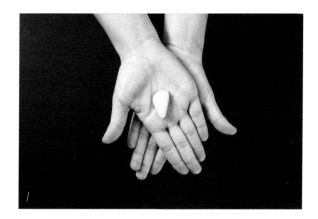

1. Take a walk in nature, focusing on the stone you are looking for and the intention you wish to set with it. Trust in fate and let yourself be carried along by your intuition to choose the one that suits you.

2. Inscribe it with a word, a phrase, a magical sign, or a personal drawing connected to the intention you wish to set (see Magical Signs and Symbols, page 144).

Magical Advice

The Power of Intention

Intention is the essential ingredient of any magical object. An object may be made with the best materials, but if no intention is set during its use or its creation, it will serve no purpose. To set an intention, all you have to do is state aloud or in your head the purpose you want to give to the object. For example: "Thank you for helping me to protect myself from negative energies" or "Thank you for helping me to have self-confidence during this important interview."

TO GO FURTHER

Lithotherapy

Due to their energetic powers, many crystals such as quartz, rose quartz, amethyst, or labradorite (to name only a few) are very powerful talismans. However, the enormous success of this practice in recent years is starting to raise real human and environmental concerns. In stores, it is difficult to verify where and how these stones were extracted. However, our regions overflow with magical minerals, such as amethyst, fluorite, quartz, or desert rose. We encourage you to learn more about where they can be found in order to go and gather them from exposed rockfaces, obviously avoiding sensitive and protected sites, or go directly to local mine operators.

Ritual
Objects

In this chapter, we present DIY projects to craft the principal ritual objects you will need to practice your magic.

During your magical work, you will come to use several ritual objects to strengthen your practice. From the magic wand to the Book of Shadows, every tool you use is an extension of yourself.

Most of these items are commercially available, especially in esoteric shops, but their effectiveness is much greater when they are made with materials carefully selected by their owner.

To be most effective, each of the objects used for your rituals and your magical work should be specifically consecrated for this purpose.

Pentacle

The pentacle is one of the most popular amulets in magic. Worn as a pendant around the neck, engraved on a cauldron, or drawn on a plaque, it is an essential tool for witches and warlocks.

The most common pentacle contains the symbol of a pentagram, a five-pointed star, represented in its circle. This tool has been used for millennia in various forms of magic. In Wiccan magic, each point represents an element. Starting from the top and moving clockwise, they represent spirit, water, fire, earth, and air. The pentacle made in this project is intended to serve you both in the consecration of objects during rituals and as a protective tool for the home.

Magical Advice

One Object, Several Uses

Consecration
The pentacle will be used for consecration during rituals. Objects to be consecrated (stones, plants, amulets, or even candles) will be placed in its center.

Protection
Hanging above an altar, a window, or a door, it will serve to protect places from negative energies.

TIP

During your rituals, you can also draw a pentacle on the ground as a magic circle. It provides protection and allows energy to be channeled during your practice. It will need to be large enough that you can sit within it. To trace it, you can use magic salt (page 88) or repositionable tape. Candles placed at each point will strengthen its power.

WHAT YOU WILL NEED

◊ 1 circle of iron or wood about 20cm (7⅞in) in diameter
◊ 1 ball of white yarn
◊ Strong glue

◊ 5 wooden branches 25cm (9⅞in) long and about 5mm (³⁄₁₆in) wide

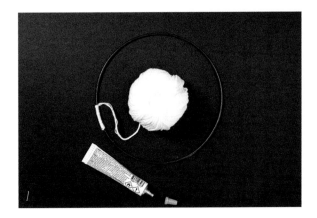

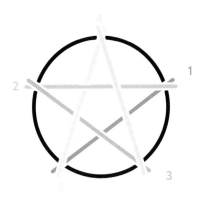

1. Wrap the white yarn around the circle until it is completely covered. Use dots of glue to fix it in place as you go.

2. Lay the wooden branches on top of the circle, following the order in the diagram (above).

3. Tie the branches and the circle together at each joint using several turns of yarn, then knot.

Tip: You can also make the circle using wire.

Magic Wand

An indispensable and loyal magical companion, the wand is a powerful tool for channeling energy and releasing it.

Used for thousands of years as an instrument of invocation in magical and religious rites, the magic wand has many functions. As a powerful channel, it directs energy to a precise point. It is also used to draw symbols or a circle on the ground. Balanced on your palm or arm, it indicates the source of danger.

But above all, your wand is an extension of yourself, a powerful tool for bringing your thoughts to life. Don't be afraid to make it your own and use it as you wish in your magical rituals. It will become your most trusted ally in channeling your magic and releasing it.

Magical Advice

Choose the wood for your wand according to its magical use.

Each tree has different properties; choose the wood for your wand according to the use you want to make of it. It is also quite possible to have several wands.

Birch	→	Healing and white magic
Oak	→	Druidry and solar magic
Willow	→	Lunar magic
Maple	→	Love
Poplar	→	Luck and prosperity
Elm	→	Protection
Hazel	→	White magic

WHAT YOU WILL NEED

◊ 1 wooden stick about 20cm (7⅞in) long
◊ Acrylic paint of your choice
◊ 1 paintbrush
◊ 1 tube of liquid glue
◊ Wool yarn in the colors of your choice
◊ 1 paint marker in the color of your choice

1. Fully paint the wand (to choose a color, see The Meaning of Colors, page 142). Let it sit until the paint is dry.

2. Determine the top and bottom part of your wand. Place a dot of glue in the center of the lower part, then place the end of the yarn on it.

3. Wind the yarn around the wand, going up along the handle. Regularly apply dots of glue to fix it in place. Stop when the covered area is the width of your hand.

4. On the upper part not covered by yarn, draw the magical symbol(s) of your choice (see Magical Signs and Symbols, page 144) using the paint marker.

Magical Advice

How do you choose your wand?
It is often said that we do not choose our wand; the wand chooses us. To find the wand that best fits, what better way than to trust in chance? Go for a walk in the woods and pick up the first straight piece of wood that draws your attention. If you can't get to the woods, a wooden stick bought from a craft store can also do the trick. Here too, we encourage you to trust your intuition in the selection process.

TO GO FURTHER

Depending on your desires, feel free to decorate your wand with elements of your choice. You can, for example, add a feather or a stone on its tip.

Smoke Cleansing Stick

The smoke cleansing stick is one of the simplest, most widely used, and most effective tools for purifying a room, person, or object.

Evidence of smoke cleansing can be found in many civilizations and religions. For a long time, it was also practiced in medicine to clean spaces that held sick patients. It can take different forms: incense, resins, or dried plants. The smoke cleansing stick is particularly widespread at this time thanks to the great success of white sage smudge sticks, used traditionally by the indigenous peoples of North and South America. While "smudging" is a culturally specific practice, smoke cleansing is done routinely as part of a personal practice and has its roots in many cultures across the globe. White sage is one of the most effective plants for cleansing and purification; however, there are many places where it is not easily grown. It's possible to find it in esoteric shops, but its success has begun to lead to production problems. Every region is full of magical plants that grow in our gardens and which can largely replace white sage. With this project, we offer recipes to make with other plants that may be easier to find.

Magical Advice

How is it used?
✧ Light one end of the stick and extinguish the flame by shaking it.
✧ To purify a place, go around each room in a counterclockwise direction, paying particular attention to the corners.
✧ To purify an object or a person, circulate the smoke from the bottom up and from the front back.
✧ To extinguish the stick, you can snuff it in sand or let it burn itself out in a heatproof container, such as a dish or a cauldron.
✧ At the end of the ritual, thank the place, the person, or the object that you have cleansed, as well as your smoke cleansing stick.

RECOMMENDATION FOR USE

Using a smoke cleansing stick is not recommended in the presence of children, pregnant women, or people with respiratory problems.

WHAT YOU WILL NEED

◊ 150g (5.3oz) of fresh plants in a bunch (10–20cm [3⅞in–7⅞in] high)
◊ 1m (1 yd) of cotton or hemp string
◊ 1 pair of scissors
◊ 1 pair of pruning shears

1. Prepare a bundle about 15cm (5⅞in) tall with all the fresh plants (must not be wet).

2. Tie a knot with the string on the lower part of the bundle, then wind the string all the way up to tie it together tightly.

3. Let your smoke cleansing stick dry by hanging it upside down for two weeks in a dry and airy place.

4. Once the plants are completely dry, untie the string (which will have loosened), then retie it tightly around your bundle. Cut off the excess string. Using your pruning shears, cut off both ends of the bundle to even out the size of the plants.

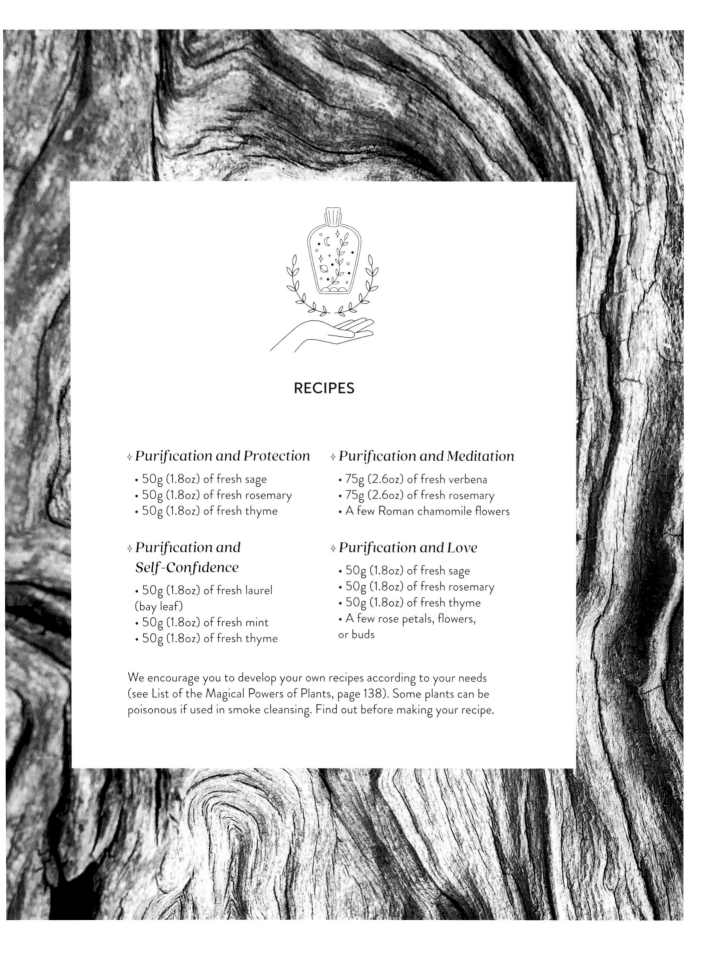

RECIPES

✧ Purification and Protection

- 50g (1.8oz) of fresh sage
- 50g (1.8oz) of fresh rosemary
- 50g (1.8oz) of fresh thyme

✧ Purification and Self-Confidence

- 50g (1.8oz) of fresh laurel (bay leaf)
- 50g (1.8oz) of fresh mint
- 50g (1.8oz) of fresh thyme

✧ Purification and Meditation

- 75g (2.6oz) of fresh verbena
- 75g (2.6oz) of fresh rosemary
- A few Roman chamomile flowers

✧ Purification and Love

- 50g (1.8oz) of fresh sage
- 50g (1.8oz) of fresh rosemary
- 50g (1.8oz) of fresh thyme
- A few rose petals, flowers, or buds

We encourage you to develop your own recipes according to your needs (see List of the Magical Powers of Plants, page 138). Some plants can be poisonous if used in smoke cleansing. Find out before making your recipe.

Magic Salt

Salt is one of the most powerful tools of purification and protection. Pure or mixed with other ingredients, it has always been used for magical work.

There are references to the use of salt in many texts, such as the Old and New Testaments, the Upanishads (in the Hindu religion), and even Homer's Iliad and Odyssey. A symbol of wisdom among the Romans, it is credited with the power to defend against negative energies in many traditions around the world. Alone or mixed with plants to strengthen and target its effects, salt is one of the most accessible and effective tools in magic.

RECIPES

✧ *Black Salt*

- 3 teaspoons of ground black pepper
- 1 teaspoon of vegetable charcoal
- 4 tablespoons of ash from plants or incense (collected when you burn incense or smoke cleansing sticks)

✧ *Green Salt*

- 2 tablespoons of dried basil
- 2 tablespoons of dried rosemary
- 2 tablespoons of dried sage
- 1 teaspoon of green oxide

✧ *Red Salt*

- A few dried rose petals
- 2 tablespoons of cayenne pepper
- 2 tablespoons of paprika
- 1 teaspoon of red oxide

WHAT YOU WILL NEED

◊ 1 mortar and pestle
◊ Ingredients depending on the type of salt
  (see Recipes, page 88)

◊ 10 tablespoons of coarse salt
◊ 1 closed container (the size of a jam jar,
  but preferably with a cork stopper)

The more natural the salt you use, the more effective it will be. Instead of refined white table salt, choose untreated salt, such as gray salt, Guérande salt, or Camargue salt.

1. Pour the salt and other ingredients into the mortar. Using the pestle, crush everything until you get a mixture of a homogeneous color.

2. Pour this mixture into the container with a cork stopper and keep it away from moisture.

USES

✦ Black Salt

Black salt is used during works of banishment, protection, or to repel a spell.
- Black salt can be used to draw a circle of protection during a magical ritual.
- You can also spread it in a line in front of windows and doors to protect a place from external energy attacks.
- A few pinches of black salt in a small vial will act as a protective amulet.

Did you know? In voodoo practices, black salt is used to counter curses.

✦ Green Salt

This magic salt draws prosperity to you. You can keep it with you in your everyday life and use it during magical rituals related to prosperity and abundance.
- Green salt can be used to make a circle of protection during a magical ritual related to prosperity.
- You can transform green salt into an amulet: Slip a few grams (about 0.14oz) of it into a folded sheet of paper, seal it with adhesive tape, and write on it what you want to see prosper. Place this amulet in your wallet.
- To bring prosperity to a whole family or to the inhabitants of a place, place the salt in a jar and place it in the house.

✦ Red Salt

Red salt is used for requests regarding love, feelings, and self-confidence.
- It is used to create a circle of protection during magical rituals related to love.
- To bring cohesion and well-being to a home, place the salt in a jar and place it in the house.
- A few pinches of red salt in a small vial will act as a love amulet.

Parchment Paper

Parchment paper is the ideal medium for writing your formulas, intentions, and requests during your rituals and magical work.

In the Middle Ages, parchment replaced papyrus in the West. Initially made from animal skin, the plant-based alternative to parchment has gradually taken its place. We present to you this project for making your parchment with recycled paper. Made yourself in mindfulness, your parchment paper will give a more powerful dimension to whatever you write on it. In particular, it will serve you during the Ostara and Litha festivals (see Pagan Festivals for Rituals, page 134) and can be used when creating talismans and amulets or when using your wish box.

Magical Advice

Seeded Paper

As suggested in the recipe, you can add seeds when making your parchment paper. By burying your seeded paper about 4cm (1½in) below the surface of some soil, the seeds will germinate and provide you with plants. Don't forget to water in order for the magic to work. This practice takes on its fullest meaning during the Ostara festival ritual (see Pagan Festivals for Rituals, page 134).

TO GO FURTHER

Magic Ink
You can write invisible messages using lemon juice or white vinegar. Use a fine brush dipped in the liquid and write your text. It can be revealed by holding your paper above a flame.

WHAT YOU WILL NEED

◊ Recycled paper, cut into small pieces (egg cartons, newspaper, scrap paper, and the like)
◊ 1 blender or immersion blender
◊ 1 basin (as large as necessary for your sieve)
◊ 1 paper sieve of the size of your choice
◊ 1 sponge
◊ 2 pieces of absorbent cloth per sheet produced (slightly larger in size than the sieve)
◊ 1 rolling pin
◊ 1 iron
◊ 1 tray

Optional: Botanical additions (flower petals, leaves, or seeds)

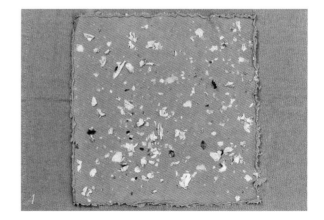

1. Place the paper in a container of very hot water for ten minutes. Mix to obtain a thick paste or pulp.

2. Pour the pulp into a basin filled with water. Immerse the sieve and collect a thin layer of the paper mixture. Leave to drain. If desired, position the botanical additions.

3. In order to remove as much water as possible from the pulp, use the sponge to gently dab first the underside of the sieve, then the surface of the pulp.

4. Using the tip of a knife, gently detach the edges of the pulp. Turn the sieve upside down and place the sheet of paper on an absorbent cloth.

5. Flatten the sheet of paper with a rolling pin. Then cover it with an absorbent cloth. Lightly run the iron over the top.

6. Place the sheets on a tray, sandwiched between 2 pieces of absorbent cloth. Place the tray on a heat source or in the sunlight for a few hours. Your parchment paper is ready when it is completely dry.

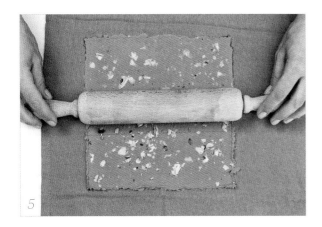

Flower Crown

**Very trendy in recent years, the flower crown is an
iconic accessory for celebrations and rituals of magic.**

Whether intended to honor the deities and the elements, displayed during victories, offered in welcome, or intended to celebrate unions, the flower crown holds an important symbolic place in many civilizations. Its use takes on its full meaning during pagan festivals that pay homage to the cycle of nature and life (see Pagan Festivals for Rituals, page 134). You can choose to make a perpetual crown made of dried flowers and foliage or a temporary crown of fresh plants.

WHAT YOU WILL NEED

◊ Metal wire
◊ 1 pair of pliers
◊ Floral tape
◊ 1 bouquet of fresh or dried flowers
  and foliage
◊ Ribbon
◊ 1 pair of scissors

Magical Advice

**Which dried plants work for
perpetual wreaths?**

✧ Baby's breath
✧ Craspedia
✧ Eucalyptus
✧ Hydrangea
✧ Lavender
✧ Peony
✧ Rose
✧ Sea lavender
✧ Thistle
✧ Wheat
✧ Yarrow

PLANT SYMBOLISM

✧ *Abundance:*
Lily, wheat

✧ *Friendship:*
Honeysuckle,
white carnation

✧ *Love:*
Fuchsia,
honeysuckle,
hyacinth, lilac,
sunflower, tulip,
white and red rose,
white camellia

✧ *Hope:*
Hawthorn,
red and yellow
anemone

✧ *Fidelity:*
Gillyflower,
ivy, speedwell,
sunflower

✧ *Joy:*
Azalea, buttercup,
crocus, hyacinth

✧ *Protection,
strength, and
power:*
Blue thistle,
gladiolus, heather

✧ *Gratitude:*
Dahlia, hydrangea

✧ *Tenderness:*
Iris, lavender,
wisteria

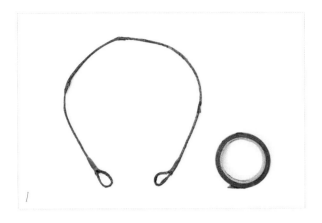

1. Cut the wire depending on the desired size of the crown. Wrap floral tape all around the wire until it is completely covered. Form 2 loops at the ends, then secure them with tape.

2. Cut small sprigs of flowers and foliage. Form small bouquets held together with tape. The quantity of these bouquets will depend on the size of your crown and the density of your plants.

3. With the tape, attach a bouquet to one end of the structure, with the flowers and leaves on the outside and stems on the inside. Then tie the next bouquet by arranging the flower/foliage part on the stems of the first, and so on.

4. Once the structure is covered with bouquets, tie the ribbons to the loops at the ends. The length of the ribbon will depend on the size of the crown and your need for adjustment.

Magic Broom

**The broom has always been the ally of witches
and a symbol of cleaning and purification.**

In popular folklore, the image of the witch and her broom flying through the air on full moon nights is one of the most common representations. We are not, however, going to present you here with instructions for creating a flying broom on which to play your next game of Quidditch. We will instead suggest that you create a "besom," an essential tool for cleaning a room before any magical work or a ritual. This sweeping will purify and protect the place by removing negative energy.

WHEN SHOULD YOU USE YOUR MAGIC BROOM?

✦ *To clean ritual spaces*
Before setting up your items for a ritual, clean the room with your broom. This helps to purify and protect the space.

✦ *To protect your home*
Place the broom at your front door, under your bed, against doorjambs, or near windows.

Note: A broom used as a magical tool must be reserved for this purpose only.

WHAT YOU WILL NEED

◊ 1 solid wood branch, at least 1m (1 yd) long
◊ 1 nail
◊ 1 hammer

◊ Thick string
◊ A few twigs or sticks (birch, wicker, broom, and
   the like)

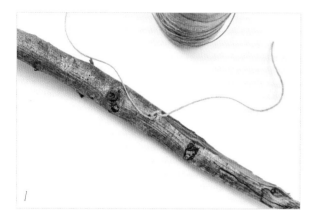

1. Drive a nail 15cm (5⅞in) from the bottom of the future broomstick. Knot the string around the nail, reserving 20cm (7⅞in) of string to make the final knot.

2. Assemble the twigs around the wooden handle. Secure them by wrapping the string several times around. To finish, knot together the 2 ends of the string.

TO GO FURTHER

Pocket Broom
To clean small spaces, you can also make a pocket broom, using the same process but using pine needles for the lower part.

Magical Advicee

Before rituals, to increase the effectiveness of your broom, rub it with chamomile, lemongrass, or elderberry.

103

Dagyde

**Made of wax, cotton, or yarn, magic dolls, also called "dagydes,"
have had a bad reputation in the collective imagination. Many people do not
know that these human representations can be used in a very positive way.**

The most famous magic practiced with dagydes is that of the voodoo tradition. However, their use is also found in Western witchcraft. They can of course be used to cast curses, but also to protect, heal, or bless. The act of representing a person allows you to better channel the magical work intended for them.

USE

During a ritual or magical work involving a particular person, place a dagyde representing them in your work area. This will strengthen the connection with that person. Dagydes can be used for work dealing with protection, healing, love, or prosperity.

Magical Advice

Once your work with the person represented by the dagyde is finished, undo the doll by untying the yarn while thanking it for the help it has given you. You can also give it to the person to whom it corresponds.

Remember
Before you make a doll as an
effigy of a person, you must
ask their permission.

WHAT YOU WILL NEED

◊ 1 ball of yarn in the color of your choice (see The Meaning of Colors, page 142)

It is possible to use several colors, depending on your needs and desires.

◊ 1 piece of cardboard, 15 × 10cm (5⅞in × 3⅞in)
◊ 1 pair of scissors

1. First, make the body: Wrap the yarn around the cardboard vertically until you have obtained a consistent mass. Remove the cardboard.

2. Make the head: On one end, tighten the threads with a knotted piece of yarn. Then, 5cm (2in) down, tie a piece of yarn to pull the mass together.

3. Make the arms: Repeat Step 1, but the mass of yarn should be less dense. To form the hands, tie pieces of yarn 2cm (¾in) from each end.

4. Assemble the body and the arms: Pass the arms through the body and connect everything with the yarn by making crossed knots.

5. Make the legs: Divide the loops of the lower part of the body. Separate the mass of the lower part of the body in halves. Then braid each of the two parts. Then, to form the feet, tie pieces of yarn 2cm (¾in) from each end.

6. To finish, cut the loops on the hands and feet. You can attach personal elements to your dagyde (a lock of hair, photo, object, or note with name and date of birth).

RECOMMENDATION

The Law of Threefold Return

Magic is a powerful tool. Everyone uses it as they see fit, but we advise you to show great benevolence toward yourself and others whenever you set an intention or make a wish. In many forms of magic, we find the Law of Threefold Return, or the Rule of Three: Each action comes back to you with three times its original force. A bad spell is often synonymous with great misfortune for the person who casts it.

Book of Shadows

The Book of Shadows is arguably the witch's or warlock's most personal object. It contains all the procedures for your magical practice.

A Book of Shadows, or "grimoire," is the confidant that will accompany you throughout your rituals and your magical work. It contains your recipes, remedies, and ritual processes, but also your commentary and experiences. You can also record your dreams and feelings there. In short, it's an upgraded diary. A Book of Shadows is an extremely personal object. It can take many forms: a nice hardcover book, a composition book, or a small notebook. The important thing is to choose a medium that you feel comfortable with and can make your own. Here we suggest that you craft your own Book of Shadows to be the perfect fit for you.

WHAT YOU WILL NEED

For an A5-sized (5⅞in × 8¼in) Book of Shadows:

◊ A4 (8¼in × 11¾in) sheets of 90 g/m² (61 lb) weight, in the color of your choice (between 25 and 150 sheets depending on the size of your Book of Shadows)

◊ Thread

◊ 1 needle

◊ 2 large books, to use as a press

◊ Strong glue

◊ 1 A2 (16⅝in × 23⅜in) sheet of 80 or 90 g/m² (55 lb or 61 lb) weight, in the color of your choice

◊ 1 piece of cardboard, about 30 × 40cm (11¾in × 15¾in)

◊ 1 ruler

◊ 1 pencil

◊ 1 craft knife

STEP 1: THE FOLIOS

1. Stack 5 A4 (8¼in × 11¾in) sheets and fold them in half. Sew the sheets together at the fold to make a small booklet or folio. Repeat the operation several times depending on the number of sheets you want to include in your book.

2. Stack the folios and press them between 2 large books. Place the glue along the spine of the future notebook to join the folios. Let dry and repeat the operation twice to fix it in place.

STEP 2: THE COVER

1. Measure the width of your book's spine. Then cut a piece of cardboard 22cm (8⅝in) × the width of the spine, then 2 other pieces of 22 × 15.3cm (8⅝in × 6in) for the cover and the back cover.

2. Glue the cover, then the spine, then the back cover on the back of your A2 (16⅝in × 23⅜in) paper, leaving a gap of 3mm (⅛in) between each section.

3. Cut off the excess paper, leaving a margin of 5cm (2in) around the covers. Then cut the corners at an angle.

4. Using liquid glue, glue the tabs down, first horizontally, then vertically.

STEP 3: ASSEMBLY

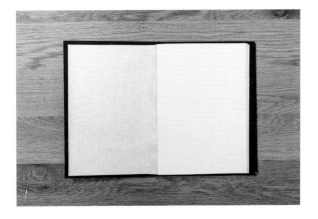

1. Glue the first interior page to the inside cover.

2. Then, glue the last page to the back cover, closing the notebook.

3. Close the book and let it dry for a few minutes. We suggest putting a heavy object on it, such as a dictionary, to keep it closed as it dries.

TO GO FURTHER

Personalize your cover with the magical symbol(s) of your choice (see Magical Signs and Symbols, page 144).

CONTENT IDEAS

⋄ *Your Profile*
Date of birth, astral chart, numerological chart, and the types of magic you practice or that interest you.

⋄ *Recipes, Remedies, and Magical Objects*
Your creations or those discovered in books or on the internet.

⋄ *Rituals*
Your rituals or those read about in books or on the internet.

⋄ *Research*
Information that you found relevant or that you want to dig into or test.

⋄ *Bibliography*
All the books you've read or want to read about magic and personal development, or that inspire you on a daily basis.

⋄ *Dreams*
Whether or not they make sense at the time.

⋄ *Dates of Pagan Festivals*
As well as the rituals to perform to celebrate them.

⋄ *Quotes and Mantras*
Also note any inspirational quotes you find as you read.

⋄ *Plants and Stones*
Document the natural magical tools that you come across along the way, as well as their properties.

⋄ *Accounts of Rituals*
What worked or didn't, and what you felt during your practices.

⋄ *Pages for Intuitive Writing*
Put your pen to paper, clear your mind, and let the pen run.

⋄ *Collages, Cuttings, and Drawings*
And whatever else you want to put in there.

Divinatory
Objects

$$\triangledown$$

In this chapter, we present a selection of magical
objects related to divination.

Complete and complex, the art of divination is one of the most
widespread magical practices. We find its traces across all civilizations,
and oracles are essential pillars of varied mythologies.

The powerful tools presented in this chapter will serve as a support
for your divination work, but they are also invaluable instruments for
developing your intuition and thus learning to know yourself better, to
grasp the world around you, and to understand it better.

Pendulum

The pendulum is a key tool in intuitive and mediumistic practices. It allows us to bring forth elements of answers not perceived by our solitary consciousness.

The practice of the pendulum is similar to that of dowsing: It makes it possible to amplify the messages perceived unconsciously by the mind and to reconstitute them using the physical body. The pendulum, therefore, becomes a form of self-extension. Its selection is specific to each person, namely that any weight hanging on the end of a wire can serve as a pendulum. However, it remains a very personal, intimate tool that should be chosen mindfully, as you would jewelry.

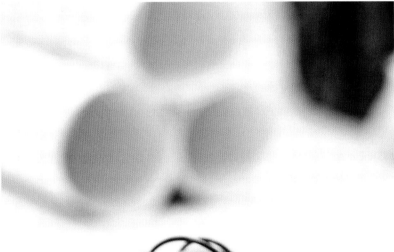

WHAT YOU WILL NEED

◊ 1 stone with a diameter of 20–25mm (¾in–1in)
◊ 1 bead cage pendant with a diameter suited to your stone
◊ 1 bead, 8–10mm (⅓in–⅜in)
◊ 1 flexible nail with a 10mm (⅜in) head
◊ 1 pair of 3-in-1 jewelry pliers
◊ 2 small, open jump rings for a fine chain
◊ 1 fine chain, 20cm (7⅞in) long

1. Insert the chosen stone into the bead cage. You can use a stone found in nature or a rough or tumbled lithotherapy stone bought in a store. It can be round or pointed—it doesn't matter.

2. Thread the bead onto the nail. Using the tip of your pliers, bend the nail and twist it so that it forms a small loop. Then, using the flat part of the pliers, tighten the loop so that it is securely closed.

3. Still using the jewelry pliers, open a jump ring and slip it into the link at the end of the chain. In this same ring, insert the loop of the bead (formed in Step 2). Close the jump ring.

4. Open the second jump ring and slip it through the link at the other end of the chain. In this same ring, insert the loop of the cage containing your stone. Close the jump ring.

HOW IS IT USED?

Hold the pendulum with your right hand (or your left if you are left-handed). Let 10cm (3⅞in) of chain hang down, held between your thumb and forefinger. Not all pendulums react the same way; you have to learn to decode the answers. To do this, during your first use, ask simple and obvious closed-ended questions, and let the pendulum act. Some pendulums will swing left to right, others back and forth; there are even some that will turn. Observe and define which movements represent "yes" and "no." Once you understand the language of your pendulum, you're all set. To use, you can either ask yes-or-no questions or use preprinted boards or boards that you have made yourself (see the model, next page). For optimal pendulum practice, the environment must be calm and your energies harmonized and aligned. To do this, take a moment to meditate and define your expectations.

BLANK BOARD

In each quarter of the blank board, you can write a possible answer to your question. Position the pendulum on the lower central part of the board, ask your question, and observe as the pendulum swings toward one of the quarters.

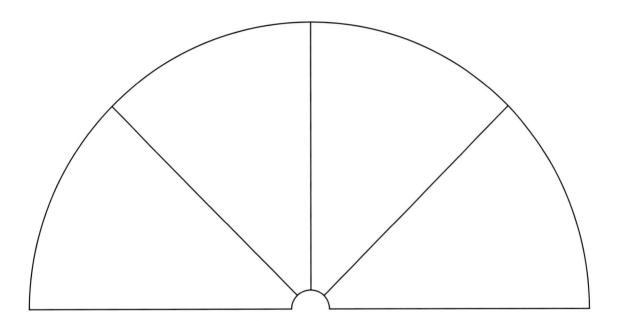

Magical Advice

Whether your choice is a rough or tumbled lithotherapy stone, or whether you have found this stone in nature, we advise you: When making your pendulum, choose an element that speaks to you intimately.

Runes

The term "runes" signifies a set of symbols releasing energies when they are drawn or visualized and through which an intention can be set.

There are several runic alphabets. The best known is the Futhark, which we will present here. It has been used by Nordic, Germanic, and English-speaking populations since the ninth century. There are also Hungarian and Turkish runic alphabets. The runic alphabet can be drawn on any medium to project an intention or to function as a divinatory tool, by inscribing each letter on a small piece of wood or a stone.

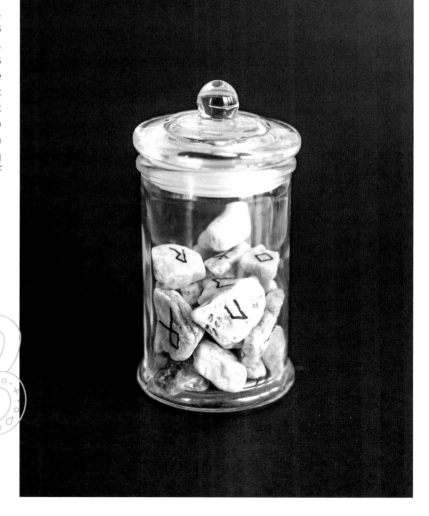

WHAT YOU WILL NEED

◊ 26 small stones (or small pieces of wood) found in nature
◊ 1 paint marker
◊ 1 small pouch

1. Write a letter of the runic alphabet on each stone. Leave one blank.

2. Keep your runes in the pouch, which you can personalize by embroidering a magical symbol or your favorite rune.

USING THE RUNES

1. Ask a question.

2. Draw 3 runes directly from the pouch.

3. Refer to the table on the next page to interpret what you have drawn.

TO GO FURTHER

There are many ways to use runes. It is a magnificent but complex art, which can be learned through long and regular practice. We suggest getting at least two books on the subject to compare different methods of using and interpreting the runes. You will be able to refine your practice and feel ownership of your runes and their meanings.

FUTHARK RUNIC ALPHABET

Fehu: Prosperity, abundance, success, health

Uruz: Power, will, courage, resilience

Thurisaz: Decision-making, action, creative energy

Ansuz: Inspiration, wisdom, communication

Raidho: Travel, action, progress, spiritual path

Kenaz: Fire, light, vision, knowledge, creation

Gebo: Generosity, gift, love, sharing

Wunjo: Joy, pleasure, harmony, comfort

Hagalaz: Air, storm, changes, transformation

Nauthiz: Trials, autonomy, acceptance, patience

Isa: Ice, challenges, hiatus, blockages

Jera: Earth, harvest, growth, evolution

Eihwaz: Transformation, rebirth, cycle change

Perthro: Femininity, mystery, magic, destiny

Algiz: Shield, protection, self-defense, warning

Sowilo: Sun, success, health, energy

Tiwaz: Duty, combativeness, justice, couragee

Berkana: Birth, beginning, liberation, novelty

Ehwaz: Team, loyalty, truth, friendship

Mannaz: Humanity, culture, collaboration, community

Laguz: Water, emotions, dream, intuition

Ingwaz: Masculinity, energy, fertility, growth

Dagaz: Day, awareness, harmony, balance

Othala: Home, heritage, ancestors, family, stability

Blank rune: The answer to the question asked is not yet known.

Oracle

The word "oracle" refers to a person endowed with the gift of divination. During the days of ancient Greece, the oracle was consulted to ask questions of the gods and to answer questions concerning the present and future.

Today, oracles come in the form of cards to help guide us. Often consulted in personal development work, they are used to predict the future, but also to learn to deepen our knowledge of ourselves. Many oracles with various themes are commercially available. It can therefore sometimes be difficult to navigate and select the one that suits us best. Making our own oracle cards allows us to build a tailor-made tool adapted to our desires and our current needs.

TIP

If you are not comfortable with drawing, you can simply write text on your cards. You can also cut out your cards and paste pictures on them. Trust your creativity.

HOW DO YOU USE YOUR ORACLE?

Single draw

The draw of a single card allows you to answer a specific question to which you want an immediate answer. You can also draw a card in the morning to find out the tone of the day to come and what you will have to work on for the next few hours.

Triple draw

You can also ask a question and draw three cards that you will place in front of you. The first signifies the past, the second the present, and the third your prospects for the future at the time the question was asked.

Complex drawings

There are many ways to draw cards (in a cross or mandala, among other options) and consult them. We encourage you to learn more about the subject and to test the different techniques to find out which one is best for you.

WHAT YOU WILL NEED

◊ Sheets of at least 200 g/m² (136 lb) weight or cards of Bristol paper
◊ 1 ruler
◊ 1 pencil

◊ 1 pair of scissors
◊ Drawing materials of your choice (markers, colored pencils, paint, and so on)

An oracle generally consists of about fifty cards.

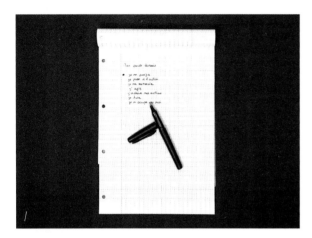

1. Select the theme of your choice and list the name of the cards that your deck will include, in order to define their number.

2. Choose a size, then trace your cards on your sheets using your ruler and pencil, or use Bristol paper cards.

3. Draw and/or write the content of your cards. Cut them out and keep them in a nice case to protect them.

THEMATIC IDEAS FOR YOUR ORACLE

✧ Inspirational quotes

✧ Mantras

✧ Nature (trees, flowers, and plants)

✧ Animals

✧ Emotions

✧ Gods

✧ Angels

✧ Tarot

✧ Astrology

✧ The Sacred Feminine

✧ Famous personalities

✧ And others

Trust your intuition to choose the theme of your oracle.

TO GO FURTHER

If you feel the need, you can write a small explanatory booklet to describe your cards, give the meaning of each, and help the people who will use your oracle with their reading.

CARD FORMATS

⬧ French format: 5.4 × 8.5cm (2⅛in × 3⅜in)
⬧ Poker format: 6.3 × 8.9cm (2½in × 3½in)
⬧ Tarot format: 6 × 11.3cm (2⅜in × 4½in), or the format of your choice (square, diamond, or why not in the shape of a star?)

Part 3

·◇·

MAGIC RESOURCES

Pagan Festivals for Rituals

AUTUMN

Element: Water
Colors: Brown, orange, purple, red, black, and blue

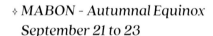

⋄ MABON - Autumnal Equinox
September 21 to 23

What we honor: The richness of the earth, abundance, and the end of harvesting.

This is the time for us to take a walk in nature, to collect elements for the altar, and to carry out energy cleansings of the home (smoke cleansing) and of the body (bath with salt and plants).

What you can place on your altar: Candles, incense or smoke cleansing sticks, fallen leaves, flowers, seasonal fruits and vegetables, wheat, wood, stones, acorns, and pine cones.

⋄ SAMHAIN
October 31 to November 1

What we honor: The dead, darkness, magic, and everything that is not visible.

This is the time for us to thank the deceased, but also the living. This is an intense period for intuition work (for example, using oracles, runes, or the pendulum).

What you can place on your altar: Candles, incense or smoke cleansing sticks, photos of and short notes to the deceased.

WINTER

Element: Earth
Colors: Red, green, and white

✧ YULE - Winter Solstice
December 21 to 23

What we honor: The longest night of the year, the return to light, the rebirth of the sun, and our loved ones.

This is the time for us to light a fire or candles and decorate a tree. We need to rest and meditate on our fears and anxieties in order to face them and visualize them in the light.

What you can place on your altar: Candles, mistletoe, holly, garlands, and gifts for your friends and loved ones.

✧ IMBOLC
February 1 to 2

What we honor: The return of light and renewed hope.

This is the time for us to meditate on our goals and how to make them a reality, to cleanse ourselves from the physical and psychic ailments of winter thanks to a purification of the home (smoke cleansing or using salt) and of the body (bath with salt and plants).

What you can put on your altar: Candles, salt, water, smoke cleansing sticks, or incense.

SPRING

Element: Air
Colors: Green, yellow, white, and pink

✧ OSTARA - Vernal Equinox
March 20 to 23

What we honor: The arrival of spring, the renewal of light, and the rebirth of nature (germination and greening).

This is the time for sowing—both literally by working the soil and planting seeds (even on a windowsill), and symbolically by writing our plans on small pieces of paper to place in a bowl on the altar or to bury in the ground.

What you can place on your altar: Candles, basket, decorated eggs, seasonal flowers, and seeds.

✧ BELTANE
April 30 to May 1

What we honor: The renewal of our own lives, joy, and expansion.

This is the time for us to meditate on the fulfillment of our projects and more generally of our lives. For example, light candles or a fire outside, make wreaths of plants, and express your joy by singing or dancing.

What you can place on your altar: Candles, seasonal flowers and fruits, elements collected from nature, and plant creations.

SUMMER

Element: Fire
Colors: White, yellow, gold, orange, pink, and green

✦ LITHA - Summer Solstice
June 20 to 22

What we honor: The climax of light, love and unity (with others, but also with oneself), energy, and joy.

This is the time for us to enjoy the longest day until the last ray of sunshine, to dance, sing, and play music (ideally around an outdoor fire), and to collect medicinal plants, fruits, and flowers.

What you can place on your altar: Candles, flowers, and seasonal plants and fruits.

✦ LUGNASAD (OR LAMMAS)
August 1 to 3

What we honor: The first harvests, our completed actions, abundance, and growth.

This is the time for us to thank the earth by making and sharing wheat-based recipes. We can also thank ourselves for our accomplished actions, whether positive or negative. Let us be grateful for the impulses and emotions that allow us to continue along our paths.

What you can place on your altar: Candles; wheat stalks; seasonal fruits, vegetables, and flowers; and bread.

List of the Magical Powers of Plants

Note: Poisonous plants were not included in this list.

✧ Abundance
Basil
Fennel
Honeysuckle
Hyssop
Lavender
Poppy
Roman chamomile
Thyme

✧ Love (of Self and of Others)
Angelica
Coriander (cilantro)
Dill
Eucalyptus
Honeysuckle
Ivy
Lavender
Roman chamomile
Rose
Thyme

Wormwood
Yarrow

✧ Anchoring
Angelica
Lovage
Pearly everlasting

✧ Aphrodisiac
Basil
Cinnamon
Coriander (cilantro)
Lemon balm
Lovage
Orange
Oregano
Rose
Sage

✧ Luck
Bergamot
Cinnamon
Dandelion
Fern
Heather
Ivy
Juniper
Laurel (bay leaf)
Mistletoe
Olive
Oregano
Poppy

Roman chamomile
Savory
Sage

✧ Communication and Social Relations
Calendula
Honeysuckle
Hyssop
Linden
Mint
Pansy
Periwinkle
Thyme

✧ Concentration
Celery
Eucalyptus
Lovage
Mint
Rosemary

✧ Courage and Strength
Angelica
Borage
Coriander (cilantro)
Dill
Garlic
Juniper
Laurel (bay leaf)
Nettle
Oak

St. John's wort
Thistle

⟡ Divination and Clairvoyance

Bird's-foot trefoil
Celery
Hazel
Heather
Laurel (bay leaf)
Lavender
Lovage
Marshmallow
Orange
Rosemary
Shepherd's purse
Wormwood

⟡ Psychic Elevation

Basil
Borage
Honeysuckle
Thyme
Wormwood

⟡ Spiritual Elevation

Angelica
Basil
Mint
Olive
Rose
Sage
Verbena

⟡ Healing (Body and Soul)

Angelica
Boxwood
Eucalyptus
Laurel (bay leaf)
Lavender
Mistletoe
Oak
Olive
Pine
Peony
Roman chamomile
Rose
Rosemary
Sage
Savory
St. John's wort
Thyme
Valerian

⟡ Harmony and Balance (Body and Mind)

Calendula
Cinnamon
Coriander (cilantro)
Eucalyptus
Honeysuckle
Lemon balm
Linden
Lovage
Orange
Pansy
Poppy
Thyme
Valerian
Yarrow

⟡ Intuition

Hazel
Laurel (bay leaf)
Lavender
Marshmallow
Orange
Rosemary
Sage
Yarrow

⟡ Inspiration and Creativity

Boxwood
Cinnamon
Eucalyptus
Juniper
Pansy
Roman chamomile
Verbena

⟡ Longevity

Lemon balm
Orange
Savory

⟡ Meditation

Lavender
Lemon balm
Roman chamomile
Rose
Sage
Verbena

⟡ Mediumship

Angelica
Olive

Thistle
Wormwood

⟡ Peace

Angelica
Dandelion
Hazel
Linden
Mallow
Mint
Oregano
Rosemary

⟡ Protection (Places and People)

Angelica
Basil
Celery
Eucalyptus
Fern
Garlic
Heather
Honeysuckle
Hyssop
Ivy
Juniper
Lavender
Lemon balm
Linden
Lovage
Mallow
Marshmallow
Mint
Mistletoe
Nettle
Oak
Olive
Oregano
Periwinkle
Pine
Roman chamomile
Rosemary
Rose

Sage
Savory
Strawberry
Thistle
Valerian
Wild thyme
Wormwood
Yarrow

◇ **Purification
(Places and People)**

Basil
Calendula
Celery
Eucalyptus
Hyssop
Laurel (bay leaf)
Lavender
Linden
Lovage

Mint
Nettle
Pine
Rosemary
Sage
Thyme
Verbena

◇ **Relaxation/Calming**

Basil
Bird's-foot trefoil
Orange
Pearly everlasting
Shepherd's purse
St. John's wort
Valerian
Verbena

◇ **Dreams**

Bird's-foot trefoil
Fern
Peony
Poppy
Wormwood

◇ **Sleep**

Heather
Lavender
Poppy
Rose
Thyme
Verbena

The Meaning of Colors

COLORS OF ELEMENTS AND CARDINAL DIRECTIONS

⬦ Blue
Element: Water
Cardinal direction: West
Peace, joy, wisdom, dreams

⬦ Yellow
Element: Air
Cardinal direction: East
Creativity, fertility, inspiration

⬦ Green
Element: Earth
Cardinal direction: North
Prosperity, abundance, luck, healing

⬦ Red
Element: Fire
Cardinal direction: South
Action, love, vitality

PRINCIPAL MAGICAL COLORS

⬦ Silver
Meditation, psychic powers, conjuration, feminine power

⬦ White
Purity, protection, balance, spirituality, renewal
(White can be a substitute for other colors.)

⬦ Ivory
Develops inspiration

⬦ Indigo
Loyalty, increases influence, clarity of mind, keeps negative energies away, meditation

⬦ Gray
Neutrality, mediation, neutralizes negative energies

⬦ Brown
Earth, prosperity, abundance, protection of animals

⬦ Mauve
Confidence, facilitates concentration and telepathy

⬦ Black
Anchoring, a link to the beyond, conjuration, protection

⬦ Gold
Luck, intuition, prosperity, confidence

⬦ Orange
Action, ambition, success, joy

⬦ Pink
Friendship, love, femininity, compassion

⬦ Violet (Mix of Blue and Red)
Psychic energies, spirituality, wisdom, divination, contact with the spirits, meditation

Magical Signs and Symbols

Goddess	Winter	Venus	Earth
God	Sun	Mars	Protection
Chalice	Moon	Jupiter	Wealth
Incense burner	Moonrise	Saturn	Travel
Cauldron	Moonset	Uranus	Healing
Pentacle	Waxing moon	Neptune	Man
Magic circle	Full moon	Pluto	Woman
Spring	Waning moon	Air	Love
Summer	New moon	Water	
Autumn	Mercury	Fire	

Lunar Phases

These lunar phases can be used for making the patterns for the Moon Mobile (page 52).

✧ **Full moon**

✧ Crescent moon ✧ Quarter moon

✧ Gibbous moon

Notes

Flos & Luna

Dear witches and warlocks,

If you liked the creations presented in this DIY book, you can find a number of them at our Flos & Luna online store. There you will discover our products, developed from plants and inspired by herbalism and magic.

Created in 2020, the Flos & Luna boutique aims to highlight the bounty of French and European magical plants. We offer smoke cleansing sticks, amulets, herbal teas, and even candles, made with love by our little hands in our cauldrons in Nantes.

You will also find the magical creations of other carefully selected French artisans.

Don't hesitate to come say hello on social media, to show us your beautiful DIY creations, and ask us all your questions.

See you soon on Flos & Luna,

Flora and Marine

From a young age, Marine Nina Denis has had a certain sensitivity and feelings. As a teenager, she became interested in the invisible and in magic. Since then, she has never stopped learning and practicing. Flora Denis was charmed by the power of plants and has been studying their benefits for physical and mental well-being for several years.

Inspired by herbalism and white, green, and Wiccan magic, these two sisters cofounded the brand Flos & Luna, offering artisanal creations to support personal and spiritual development.

Website: flosetluna.fr
Instagram: @flosetluna
Facebook: /flosetluna

THANKS

Thanks to Chloé, our favorite editor, for her confidence and her light.

Thank you to all the witches and wizards who cross our paths, and also to all those who do not practice magic and who inspire us with their talents.

Thanks to Benoit, Cassandre, Jonathan, Kelso, Lucie, and Martin for brightening our daily lives.

METRIC CONVERSIONS

The metric measurements in this book follow standard conversion practices for sewing and soft crafts. The metric equivalents are often rounded off for ease of use. If you need more exact measurements, there are a number of amazing online converters.

DIY for Witches

First published in the United States in 2022 by Stash Books, an imprint of C&T Publishing, Inc., P.O. Box 1456, Lafayette, CA 94549

© First published in French by Secret d'étoiles, Paris, France—2021

www.secretdetoiles.com

This edition of "Le grand livre du DIY de sorcière" first published in France by Secret d'étoiles in 2021 is published by arrangement with Fleurus Éditions.

PUBLISHER: Amy Barrett-Daffin
CREATIVE DIRECTOR: Gailen Runge
ACQUISITIONS EDITOR: Roxane Cerda
ASSOCIATE EDITOR: Jennifer Warren
ENGLISH-LANGUAGE COVER DESIGNER: April Mostek
ENGLISH TRANSLATION: Kristy Darling Finder
ILLUSTRATORS: Yana Bolbot and Laurent Stéfano (pages 39 and 145)
PHOTOGRAPHER: Benoit Beghyn
GRAPHIC ELEMENTS: ©iStock

Printed in the USA

10 9 8 7 6 5 4 3 2